# Tranquilizers

Lawrence Clayton, Ph.D.

## —The Drug Library—

**Enslow Publishers, Inc.**

| | |
|---|---|
| 44 Fadem Road | PO Box 38 |
| Box 699 | Aldershot |
| Springfield, NJ 07081 | Hants GU12 6BP |
| USA | UK |

*To the faculty and students at Mid-America Bible College.*

Copyright © 1997 by Lawrence Clayton, Ph.D.

**Library of Congress Cataloging-in-Publication Data**

Clayton, L. (Lawrence)
    Tranquilizers / Lawrence Clayton.
      p. cm. — (The drug library)
    Includes bibliographical references and index.
    Summary: Discusses the history, effects, use, and abuse of tranquilizers.
    ISBN 0-89490-849-9
    1. Tranquilizing drugs—Juvenile literature. [1. Tranquilizing drugs. 2. Drug abuse.] I. Title. II. Series.
    RM333.C53   1997
    615'.7882—DC20              96-26949
                                       CIP
                                       AC

Printed in the United States of America

10 9 8 7 6 5 4 3 2 1

**Photo Credits:** Linda Berryman of As You Wish Photography, pp. 7, 11, 21, 31, 38, 45, 48, 52, 60, 74, 76; Rob Roddy, pp. 43, 47.

**Cover Photo:** Enslow Publishers, Inc.

# Contents

# Acknowledgments

I would especially like to thank the employees of the Lawton, Oklahoma and the Edmond, Oklahoma Public Libraries for their help in digging through mounds of magazine and journal articles for me. Their help was as invaluable as it was time-consuming. I would also like to thank my children, Larry and Rebecca, for their help in sorting through the above pieces of research to find those articles which were just right for this book. They gave up a good deal of their own time to be of service to me and, through this, to others.

I would like to express my gratitude to Rob Roddy for his courage in coming forward to reveal his personal struggle with tranquilizers. Although he has already done this in schools and churches, it was a giant step for him to do so for a larger audience. My deepest grateful acknowledgment and appreciation is given to Linda Berryman, owner of As You Wish Photography for her excellent photographs. She has contributed almost all of the photographs found in this volume. In doing so, she has gone to great lengths in order to do her very best work for this book. The quality of her professionalism is evident in the clarity of her work.

Thanks, guys!

# 1
# History of Depressants: Use and Abuse

Tranquilizers belong to a classification of drugs commonly referred to as depressants. These drugs are actually poisons that depress or slow down the body and mind. Like all poisons, if they are used in a large enough dose, death will result. But these drugs are more deadly than most. In fact, depressants are so dangerous that they are the leading cause of accidental poisoning in the world.[1] Depressants are particularly deadly when used in combination with one another, especially if one of them is alcohol.

When a depressant enters the body, it lowers the rate at which the heart beats, the lungs breathe, the brain thinks, and the body reacts. Depressants also lower blood pressure and metabolism (the chemical processes by which cells in the human body produce the energy necessary for life). This is why many tranquilizer addicts are overweight. Depressants make people relax, dull their feelings, and give them a sense that everything is right with the world. If too much of the drug is used (called an overdose) and the bodily functions become too depressed, they simply stop. That means the heart will stop beating, the lungs will quit breathing, the brain will stop thinking, the body will stop reacting, and the person will die. All depressants affect people in this way.[2] For more about how tranquilizers effect the body, please refer to Chapter 3.

Depressants kill thousands of people every year, including many celebrities. Depressants have played a part in the deaths of Elvis Presley, Marilyn Monroe, and River Phoenix.[3] Many other celebrities have been addicted to them, including Michael Jackson, former first lady Betty Ford, Liza Minelli, Elizabeth Taylor, and Barbara Gordon (a 1960s movie producer who wrote a book about her experience with tranquilizers).[4]

There are four main types of depressants: alcoholic beverages, narcotics, barbiturates, and tranquilizers.[5] While each of these drugs has its own unique history, there are also some surprising similarities among them, not the least of which is that they are cross-addictive. That is, depressant addicts will use another depressant when their drug of choice in not available.

### Alcohol

Alcohol was first used in ancient times. According to authors Ray and Ksir an ancient beverage called "mead," which was made from fermented honey, was the oldest known alcoholic substance in the world and was first mentioned in history about 8000 B.C.[6]

6

Alcohol is the world's oldest drug. It has been used in one form or another since about 8000 B.C. Ancient writings describe drinkers as saying, "If it lays me out flat, what do I care? As soon as I wake up I will return to my wine."

Very little else is known about this drink, except that it was quite popular and caused a lot of problems for those who drank it.

Beer, which is about 4 percent alcohol, dates from about 6400 B.C. and seems to have been used throughout the known world, even in the Western Hemisphere.[7] Contrary to popular belief, European explorers and settlers did not introduce the Native Americans to alcohol. In fact, Native Americans were drinking beer long before Columbus discovered America.[8] What the Europeans brought over was distilled alcohol, which was a lot stronger than beer.

Wine was first made by the Egyptians about 4000 B.C. Stone writing tablets have been found in ancient Egyptian tombs that describe the process of wine making in great detail.[9] Wine is about 12 percent alcohol, or three times stronger than beer.[10] Like all depressants, this beverage was consumed in order to help people relax and sleep, and many became addicted to it. Wine also caused major personality problems for users and many social problems were associated with its use.

Many of those who drank too much wine became loud, abusive, and angry. Some even acted out sexually and failed to support their children.[11] Many of them drank so much that they could not think, walk, or talk correctly. They would often continue to drink until they lost control of their bodies and their minds. Some people would actually hallucinate (see, hear, smell, taste, or feel things that are not really there). If they continued to drink, they would eventually become unconscious (also called "passing out," which actually means to go into an alcohol-induced coma). Some got so confused they could not even remember what had happened to them while they were drinking. They blacked out.[12]

The writer of one of the books of the Bible called Proverbs (which was written about 2500 B.C.) knew the damaging impact of alcohol and its addictive nature and warned people about it:

> *Who is miserable? Who is remorseful? Who has quarrels and is anxious? Who gets bruises without knowing why? Who has bloodshot eyes? The man who lingers over wine, he who is always trying some new spiced liquor. Beware of the wine . . . in the end it will bite you like a snake. Then you will see strange things, your wits and your speech will be confused . . . and you will stagger about like a man on a ship at sea. You will say, "If it lays me out flat, what do I care? . . . As soon as I wake up, I will return to my wine."*[13]

These problems became even worse starting in about A.D. 1000 with the invention of the process of distillation, a process that greatly increases the amount of alcohol in a beverage.[14] This new process led to the production of whiskey, brandy, vodka, gin, and rum which are each about 50 percent alcohol, which is over four times the amount of alcohol in wine and over ten times the amount of alcohol in beer.[15] The problems associated with these new spirits were even more severe than those previously caused by wine and beer.

## Narcotics

The first known mention of narcotic use was about 4000 B.C. An ancient people called Sumarians (who lived in what is now Iraq) used opium to "dull all pain and anger and bring forgetfulness of every sorrow."[16] They had problems because of it.

Some of the problems were that some opium addicts gained weight and got lazy, forgot about working, did not take good care of their children, and often slept through the day. Some people also tended to do poorly at work and forgot other important events.[17] The writer of "The Five Precepts," a major part of the Buddhist religion, knew how dangerous opium was and required the people to promise that they would not use these intoxicants (drugs):

> *The Five Precepts which are incumbent on every Buddhist,*
> *are to abstain [to completely refrain] from killing, stealing,*
> *sex outside marriage, lying and intoxicants.*[18]

Morphine is a narcotic that was developed in 1803 by a German pharmacist named F. W. Serturner. A very powerful drug, it is ten times stronger than opium.[19] Scientists initially thought it was not addictive, so doctors began prescribing it to the public as a cure for opium addiction.[20] They also prescribed it for control of pain. Many doctors believed it was the best pain medication ever developed. No one thought it would soon kill people. Sir William Osler, a Canadian physician, even went so far as to call it "God's Own Medicine."[21]

Then, in 1855, something happened to change the way morphine was used. The hypodermic needle was invented. This made morphine easy to use in large amounts and caused it to become the drug of choice for thousands of addicts.[22]

During the American Civil War, doctors prescribed morphine to soldiers for everything from headaches and stomachaches to nervousness. It was also used for pain related to battlefield wounds. The result was that over four hundred thousand soldiers became addicts.[23] In fact, morphine addiction was so common among Civil War veterans that it was commonly called "The Soldier's Disease."[24]

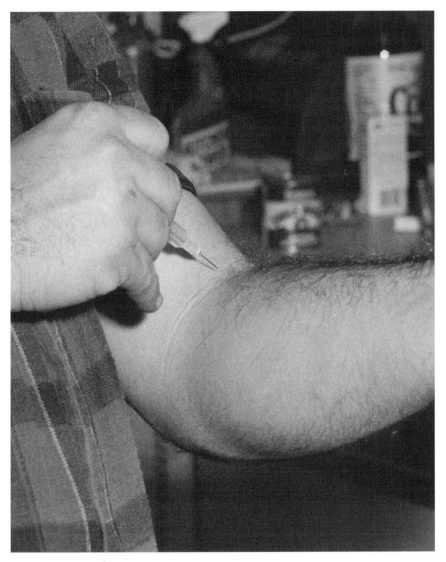

With the invention of the hypodermic needle, morphine addicts were able to administer large doses of the drug directly into the bloodstream.

In 1898 the Beyer Company introduced a new drug that it claimed would do everything that morphine did without getting people addicted. In fact, this new drug was said to end morphine addiction and alcoholism forever.[25] The press called it the "hero drug." Beyer simply called it heroin. It became the most addictive medication the world had ever known. By 1920, it was perceived to be the country's major drug problem.[26] Today, there are over two million heroin addicts in the United States alone.[27]

## Barbiturates

Back in 1864 a different kind of depressant had been discovered. It seems a German scientist named Beyer, the same man who invented heroin, had mixed apple acid with human urine and got a substance that he named "barbituric" in honor of a Munich waitress named Barbara who had given him samples of her urine for his experiments. (In this way, "Barbara's urates" became "barbiturates.")[28] Almost forty years later, scientists Emil Fischer and Joseph Von Mering discovered that barbiturates were helpful in treating pain, sleeplessness, and nervousness. They also believed, as did most other scientists and doctors, that these new drugs were not addictive and would end both heroin addiction and alcoholism forever.[29]

Doctors prescribed barbiturates and pharmacies sold these medications by the millions. The companies that manufactured them were made wealthy beyond their wildest dreams—making millions of dollars in the process. This started a whole new wave of research. Scientists and pharmaceutical companies, hoping to cash in on the consumer demand for more of these drugs, developed over twenty-seven hundred different types of barbiturates.[30]

As you might expect, doctors soon discovered that there were millions of people addicted to barbiturates. Edward Becher, a social worker, pointed out that barbiturate addicts acted just like alcoholics and heroin addicts (which is not surprising, since barbiturates are just another kind of depressant):

> *They neglected their appearance, became unkempt and dirty, did not shave, bathed infrequently and allowed their living quarters to become filthy. They were content to wear clothes soiled with food which they had spilled. All patients were confused and had trouble performing simple tasks. . . . While drunk on barbiturates, they became quarrelsome and irritable. They cursed each other, and at times even fought violently.[31]*

Once again, the medications that were thought to be nonaddictive were discovered to be just the opposite. While they were effective for some problems, these drugs provided no magic cure. In many cases, the abuse and addiction they caused created problems far worse than the ones for which they were effective. For all of science's hard work of searching for the perfect depressant, no such drug had been found. At this point the world was ready for a new "magic bullet." That magic bullet would be the tranquilizer.

# Questions for Discussion

1. The drugs we have discussed in this chapter can do serious damage to people. They can also be helpful to people. How would you know if it was all right to use one of these drugs?

2. We in the United States have often been critical of foreign governments' failure to control drug trafficking in their countries. Have we done any better in ours?

3. In the past, doctors seemed willing to believe that a new drug was not addictive. They also seemed to be the first ones to find out that the new drug was addictive. Why do you think this is so? Would you rely on a doctor to tell you if a drug is addictive? If not, who would you trust?

# 2

# "Mother's Little Helper"

In 1954 a new type of depressant was discovered.[1] The scientific community once again believed it had found the perfect depressant medication. It was even said to be safe to use while driving a car. It was supposed to be very relaxing and able to soothe the most severe anxieties. At this time, it was also mistakenly said to be nonaddictive. In addition, it proved to be extremely effective as a painkiller. The scientific name for this new drug was meprobamate. It was marketed to the world under its brand name, Miltown™. Because of its tranquilizing effect on users, most people began calling it a "tranquilizer." The name caught on and this class of drugs has been so called ever since. Soon people discovered that tranquilizers were great fun and "Miltown parties," where people got together for the sole purpose of using the drug, were very popular.[2] People who used it reported that they felt very calm, at peace, and experienced little or no pain. They also reported feeling very happy and satisfied with their lives and with those around them.[3]

However, to fully understand how this new drug became so popular in our society, it is important to understand the situation facing the medical community at the time it was developed. Doctors had prescribed billions of doses of the depressants, largely narcotics and barbiturates, to people. These medications all had serious side effects, including the fact that they were highly addictive.[4]

To complicate matters, some of these depressants were not effective for the purposes for which they were prescribed. The *High Times Encyclopedia of Psychoactive Drugs* describes the dilemma facing both the public and the medical community:

> There were a plethora of sleeping aids and nerve tonics in use at the turn of the twentieth century. Doctors prescribed alcohol in extravagant quantities, also with various preparations of opium . . . and other depressants. But each of these had their drawbacks, it was noted in clinical use. Alcohol was not a proper remedy for teetotalers or lushes; chloral hydrate and paraldehyde were unpleasant to take; bromides were toxic, opiates addicting.[5]

Millions of unsuspecting people became addicted to these drugs. Tranquilizers seemed to offer a solution. Perhaps this is the reason so many doctors and patients readily accepted the claims that these drugs were harmless.

The medical establishment welcomed tranquilizers and began prescribing them by the millions to their patients. Doctors believed they were finally able to provide effective help with few side effects to people who suffered from pain, sleeplessness, and anxiety.

In addition, this was a very profitable business for the drug companies, who responded by spending unprecedented amounts of money advertising tranquilizers. Of course, their financial successes also created a new wave of research and by 1960 several new tranquilizers were put on the market.

The most important of these was Librium™. It was the first widely used tranquilizer and doctors, believing that it was non-addictive, wrote record numbers of prescriptions for it.

They prescribed it, largely to women, for everything from menstrual cramps to anxiety.[6] However, it had an extremely high addictive potential. Because of its positive qualities, it quickly became the most prescribed drug in the entire world.[7]

Doctors even began prescribing it to treat alcoholics. In the end, their mistake was realized: "When the alcoholics drank less, they thought they had achieved a cure, but all they had really done was to substitute one . . . drug for another."[8] In fact one expert called it "whiskey in a pill."[9] (For more about this see the discussion of cross-tolerance in chapter 3.)

Valium™ was introduced in 1963.[10] It, too, was thought to be a safe, nonaddictive substitute this time, for Miltown and Librium as well as for the barbiturates. Many other tranquilizers were introduced during this period including Triazopam™, Prazepam™, Ativan™, Halasepam™, Temazepam™, Oxazepam™, and Clorazepate™. With the sole exception of Ativan, none of these was widely used. But Valium became the drug of choice for millions of women. In fact this drug was used by so many women that it was commonly referred to as "Mother's Little Helper." The Rolling Stones, a popular rock band at that time, recorded a song by that name in July 1966.[11]

Valium use was so widespread that it soon replaced Librium as the world's most prescribed drug. Unlike Miltown, it was available in both pill and injectable forms. For those who became addicted quickly, this made it simple to begin mainlining (using a needle to inject the drug directly into the veins).[12] Meanwhile, most abusers continued to take the drug in pill form. By 1976 some thirty million Americans were consuming three billion Valium tablets a year.[13] It soon became evident that many more people were using Valium than had ever used Librium, another dilemma for the medical establishment.

A few years later in 1981, another tranquilizer, called Xanax[TM], was put on the market. One more time, scientists stated that this drug was a nonaddictive substitute for its forerunners. Because of the level of abuse and addiction to Librium and Valium, the world was by now in need of a new, safe alternative.

To illustrate the desperateness with which our country and government viewed the Valium problem, Xanax was approved by the United States Food and Drug Administration (USFDA) and prescribed to millions of people without its manufacturer having ever completed its required preliminary tests of the drug. This was the first time in history that the USFDA approved a drug before its preliminary trials were finished.[14] Unfortunately, history once again repeated itself: when those tests were completed, scores of researchers concluded that Xanax was an addictive drug. During those trials it was revealed that 57 percent of people who used Xanax for up to three months could not quit. Compared to

Valium, it had a far greater addictive potential. In another test, which has been used as a comparison to the above study, only 29 percent of those who used Valium for an equivalent three month period had difficulty stopping their use of the drug.[15]

Among the withdrawal symptoms associated with stopping the use of Xanax are the following: severe anxiety, sweating, tachycardia (rapid heartbeat), sleeplessness, chronic blinking, agitation, rage, rigid muscles, seizures, hallucinations, disorientation, shock, elevated blood pressure, and heart failure.[16]

Even so, there are still doctors who believe that Xanax is harmless that "you could take a whole bottle and all you would do is fall asleep."[17] Studies in Canada, however, revealed that those patients who used Xanax for eight weeks actually had higher levels of anxiety than when they first started using the drug.[18] Despite this, and largely due to an extensive marketing plan, Xanax sales skyrocketed and by 1987 it was the world's most prescribed drug.[19]

That same year researchers were sending warnings to doctors about the dangers of Xanax withdrawal. They were saying that stopping this drug after prolonged use could cause people to have convulsions, go temporarily insane, and experience a return of the symptoms such as anxiety for which they had originally started taking the drug.[20] Despite all of this, Xanax is still the world's most prescribed psychoactive drug (one that affects emotions).[21]

Tranquilizers are also one of the most dangerous classes of drugs, so dangerous that they are listed as controlled substances in both the United States and Canada.[22] They are highly addictive. By 1985 over fifty-one million Americans were using tranquilizers and 350 million prescriptions a year were written for them. This is over sixty doses for every man, woman, and child in the United States.[23]

Numerous cases of accidental poisoning were also being reported, many of them due to the compounding effect of tranquilizers and alcohol. It seems that whenever these drugs and any other depressant are used together, the effect is multiplied. This has been a major problem in the United States for many years. In fact, the National Institute on Drug Abuse Prevention says that during a one-year period, forty-seven thousand people were rushed to emergency rooms because they mixed a barbiturate or tranquilizer with alcohol. Twenty-five hundred of them died.[24]

Tranquilizers are also very deadly when taken in a manner in which they are not prescribed. Like most drugs, the body builds up tolerance to tranquilizers, so they become increasingly ineffective. Users often respond by taking more. This brings them a step closer to an overdose each time they increase the level of their use.

Also, many children have been poisoned because they found a bottle of tranquilizers and ate too many of them. These are very powerful drugs. As The National Child Safety Council has pointed out, "one pill might induce sleep, five pills can result in coma and ten pills can result in death."[25]

Even so, addicts often use tranquilizers and alcohol together because of the interactive effect. They also use them with other drugs such as marijuana, barbiturates, and heroin.[26] All such combinations are potentially fatal.

It should not be thought that tranquilizers are only a problem in the United States. They are also a problem in many other countries as well. For example, in Ontario, Canada, during 1977

Careless handling of tranquilizers has led to many accidental poisonings of children. These are extremely dangerous drugs and should be kept in a safe place.

(the most recent data available), 47.6 percent of the population acknowleged using tranquilizers.[27]

Attempts to control tranquilizer misuse, abuse, and addiction have been largely unsuccessful. Some states, such as Oklahoma, have begun monitoring doctors' prescriptions of tranquilizers, hoping to catch the so-called "script doctors," who knowingly prescribe to drug abusers.[28]

To make matters worse, almost half as many people as use prescribed tranquilizers are using illegal or street tranquilizers, according to the government's own research. Some of these drugs are made in illegal drug labs, while others are smuggled in from Mexico, where they can be purchased from drugstores without a prescription.[29]

In the meantime, "one out of every six Americans takes a tranquilizer every day," and they are the world's most widely abused prescription drug, not only in the United States and Canada, but also in Europe and Japan.[30] Three tranquilizers, Librium, Valium, and Xanax, together are still the world's most prescribed drugs.[31]

Among young adults, tranquilizer abuse has been increasing for several years and is now the fourth leading drug of abuse after alcohol, cocaine, and marijuana.[32] Every year, teens throughout the country, who are largely unaware of the dangers, risk sickness or death when they combine tranquilizers and alcohol.

# Questions for Discussion

1. What is the difference between tranquilizer use and tranquilizer abuse?

2. What would you do if you began to have severe problems with anxiety?

3. What advice would you give someone if you knew he or she was taking prescribed tranquilizers and someone offered him or her a beer?

# 3

# How Tranquilizers Work

In order to comprehend how tranquilizers impact the body and mind of the user, it is necessary to understand the route these chemicals follow once they enter the body. It is also important to understand the normal function of the various parts of the body and brain that are encountered by tranquilizers as they make their journey through the body.

Next, analysis of how tranquilizers impact the various organs of the body and the parts of the brain that they encounter is needed. After looking at these dynamics, the appropriate uses of tranquilizers will be discussed, including how and why they are effective in treating a variety of medical problems. At that point, a closer look will be taken at what happens in the body and brain of someone who abuses or becomes addicted to tranquilizers.

## Tranquilizers' Journey Through the Body

Most tranquilizers enter the body through the mouth, although some, like Valium, can be injected.[1] Injectable tranquilizers, however, are somewhat difficult to obtain, transport, and store, and they are not as convenient to use. Those that are taken orally are digested in the stomach and intestines. Then they are absorbed through the intestinal walls directly into the bloodstream. Once in the bloodstream, they are transported to the liver where they are metabolized (broken down into usable components). About 85 percent of those components attach themselves to proteins in the blood.[2] The remainder attach themselves to blood sugars and acids. In this form, they are transported through the bloodstream to the brain, where they make their impact.

Once in the brain, tranquilizers begin depressing all general brain functions. Some of the more important areas of the brain that are impacted are the thalamus, the cerebral cortex, the hypothalamus, and the frontal lobes.

The thalamus is the portion of the brain that functions as a receiving and communicating center. It accepts messages related to such things as pleasure, pain, heat, and cold from various parts of the body. Then, acting like a telephone switchboard, it sends these messages to other parts of the brain including the cerebral cortex.[3]

The cerebral cortex is the part of the brain that functions as the sensation processing center of the brain. It processes visual, auditory, olfactory (smell), and gustatory (taste) signals. It also controls involuntary muscle movement such as breathing, heartbeat, and muscle spasms, and it translates messages from the thalamus, sending many of them on to the hypothalamus.[4]

The hypothalamus controls our reactions to the outside world. This is the part of the brain that experiences anger, fear, and anxiety. It also regulates bodily functions related to these emotions. When the hypothalamus experiences anger or fear, it reacts by causing large amounts of the blood to flow from the arms and legs and to gather in the center of the body and in the head. This is called the flight/fight response because it protects people in emergencies by making it harder for them to bleed to death if one of their limbs is cut or torn away. This also enables them to think more clearly by forcing higher than usual amounts of oxygen-rich blood into their brains.[5] In addition, the hypothalamus sends impulses directly to the frontal lobes of the brain.

Just how the frontal lobes work is still somewhat of a mystery. What we do know is that they are the site of the major inhibitors, also known as the conscience. These highly complex organs are part of what separates the human being from other animals who cannot experience guilt. They are also where a good deal of judgment and thought formation occurs.[6] People who have damaged frontal lobes may not have any experience of guilt, may be highly impulsive, and may have severely impaired judgement.

After having made their impact on the brain, tranquilizers continue their journey in the bloodstream through the rest of the body to the kidneys. There they are processed into urine and transported to the bladder to be expelled from the body.[7] It is important to understand that tranquilizers have an impact on every part of the body and brain that they encounter.

## Medical Uses of Tranquilizers

Tranquilizers are used by medical professionals, medical doctors (MDs), doctors of osteopathy (DOs), chiropractors (DCs), and dentists (DDSs) to help patients suffering from numerous medical difficulties. These drugs can be effective in treating many medical problems. Just what these problems are and how tranquilizers can have a useful impact on them will be discussed next.

## Seizures

A seizure is an involuntary contraction of the body's muscles. This is caused when the electrical impulses in the brain begin a sudden and extremely intense discharge. This, in turn, causes the thalamus to send messages to the muscles telling them to react.[8]

There are several types of seizures. When someone has a petite mal seizure, he or she simply loses control of his or her muscles for a brief time, usually only a second or two. This happens so fast that most people will not realize that a seizure has occurred. The person who is having the seizure usually slumps momentarily and his or her eyelids may flutter. However, when someone has a grand mal seizure, he or she generally loses all control of muscles for an extended period of time. He or she usually falls to the floor twitching, shaking, and jerking. This can be very frightening to the victim as well as to onlookers.

Tranquilizers are often recommended for seizure victims because they tend to slow down the firing of the brain's electrical impulses. This often helps the seizure victim gain control of his or her body. Continued use of tranquilizers may even be effective in preventing future seizure episodes.[9]

27

## Muscle Spasms

During and after intense exercise or when a muscle is overextended, the muscle can respond by starting to spasm (to contract rhythmically). This can be extremely painful and makes moving the muscle difficult, if not impossible. The muscle actually begins to function by itself. In other words, the brain loses control of the muscle.

Tranquilizers can help control muscle spasms by regulating the nerve impulses in the brain that normally control muscle movement. They do this in much the same way as they control the brain's seizure activity, by slowing down the electrical charges in the cerebral cortex.[10] This, in turn, can help the brain regain control of the muscles and frequently provides relief for those who are experiencing muscle spasms.

## Anxiety

Anxiety is a term used to describe the state of a person who is chronically worried or fearful. In some ways, anxiety is the result of being in the flight/fight state for too long of a time, especially when there is nothing to fight with or flee from. It is like experiencing the fear of being attacked when no threat is near.

When that happens the heart beats faster, blood pressure goes up, the lungs breathe deeper, and the blood rushes to the brain and to the center of the body. While this has certain advantages, it can also be dangerous if it continues for an extended period of time. Some of the disadvantages are exhaustion and the possibility of a stroke or heart attack.[11]

Tranquilizers can help those who are anxious by slowing brain and body functions, thereby allowing the anxious person to relax. They do this by slowing the firing of the electrical impulses in the hypothalamus.[12]

## Sleep Problems

There are times when people have difficulty sleeping. Some of this may be caused by anxiety. At other times, it may be caused depression, alcohol or other drug abuse, eating too much sugary food, drinking beverages containing caffeine, or by doing intense hard work or exercise just before bedtime.[13] While some of these problems can be successfully dealt with by a change in habits or diet, others cannot.

Tranquilizers have proven to be effective in lowering anxiety. They can also be helpful in allowing the mind to slow down long enough to enable most people to fall asleep.[14]

## Pain

Tranquilizers are also useful in helping people deal with various kinds of pain. In order to understand how tranquilizers do this, one must first understand how the experience of pain happens in the body and within the brain. The skin and many other tissues have numerous pain receptors that are programmed to interpret pain impulses. Whenever one of these receptor cells is stimulated by some kind of damage, either to themselves or to nearby cells, the fibers in these cells transmit pain impulses to the brain. They do this by stimulating one of two types of fibers designed to transmit messages to the thalamus. "A" fibers are very quick transmitters that carry messages relating to sharp pain. "C" fibers transmit more slowly and carry messages of dull pain such as burning, itching, or aching.[15]

29

Tranquilizers can be effective when either of these kinds of pain becomes unbearable. They do this by blocking the pain impulses just as they reach the thalamus. This stops the pain impulses from being transmitted to the rest of the brain.

## How People Become Addicted to Tranquilizers

The overwhelming majority of people who become addicted to tranquilizers are already abusing some form of drug, usually another depressant such as alcohol, narcotics, or barbiturates.[16] Then, they are exposed to tranquilizers. Soon, they find that tranquilizers are easy to use and give them much the same feeling as the other depressants gave them, but often with fewer side effects. They may have been introduced to tranquilizers by a friend who uses drugs or by a medical professional who was treating them for one of the medical problems described earlier.

In the beginning, those who were already abusing depressants probably started occasionally substituting a tranquilizer for the other drug. Then, when they discovered it worked just as well, they used any depressant they could get. This is called "cross-addiction"—any of the depressants work just as well for them.[17]

This is usually followed by the abuser becoming increasingly attracted to the tranquilizers, to the exclusion of the other drug. This state is often referred to as "primary tranquilizer addiction."

Others may follow a different route on the way to tranquilizer addiction. These people may not have been abusing drugs at all. They simply had a medical problem. They were in pain, overly anxious, having seizures or muscle spasms, or just could not get

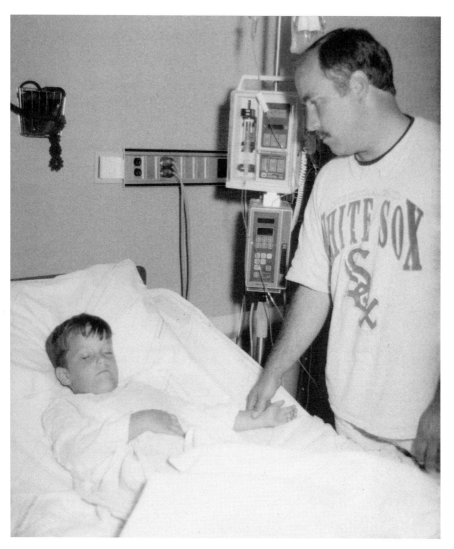

Children are so small and tranquilizers are so powerful that one pill can put them to sleep, five can result in the child slipping into a coma, and ten can result in death.

the sleep they needed. Whatever the problem, it got so bad they sought medical help and the doctor prescribed tranquilizers.

Initially, the person liked the way tranquilizers made him or her feel. In other words, the tranquilizers were effective for the medical problem. After a time, however, the tranquilizers did not work as well. The pain returned, the anxiety got worse, the seizures came back, the muscle spasms started all over, or sleep was hard to get. The user's body and brain had become used to the drug.

At that point, the person started using a larger dose of the tranquilizers. Once again the tranquilizers were effective. This is called tolerance and is one of the first symptoms of addiction.[18]

Some merely discovered that by increasing the dosage the tranquilizers became effective once again. Others found that if they mixed tranquilizers and alcohol, the tranquilizers worked better. This combination is particularly dangerous, being the leading cause of accidental poisoning in the United States.

In either case, those who continued to increase the dosage without appropriate medical supervision or who mixed tranquilizers with alcohol were often destined to become addicted. That is, they found themselves to be in emotional and physical pain when they tried to cut back or stop using this drug. This makes it difficult, if not impossible, for them to discontinue the drug. Many never do. Some simply continue using them until they die.

## What Happens to People Who Abuse Tranquilizers

Tranquilizers have a horrible impact on the minds and bodies of those who abuse them. Almost as soon as these drugs enter the body, they begin changing the way the brain functions. As you know by now, this can be beneficial if tranquilizers are used as medically prescribed.

The problem is that few people who use these drugs for very long are able to use them appropriately. Many people find they have difficulty discontinuing tranquilizer use in as little as three months. This has prompted the American Medical Association to recommend against prescribing tranquilizers for extended periods of time.[19]

As the addict continues to abuse tranquilizers, he or she will continue to increase the dosage or take them with other depressants. This is because of tolerance (as discussed earlier). Unfortunately, many people mistakenly think that people with a large tolerance to a drug can take as much of that drug as they would like. There is, however, a point for every person, no matter how experienced, at which these drugs become toxic. Remember, the only difference between a depressant and a poison is the dose.

Tranquilizers, as we have seen, also impact the hypothalamus, the part of the brain that normally triggers the flight/fight response. When someone takes a tranquilizer, blood pressure falls, blood vessels are dilated, and the heart must beat faster and harder. After a time, the heart can start to race and beat irregularly and the volume of blood can slow.[20] This will impact the kidneys, which begin shutting down. They will quit filtering the blood, and uric nitrogen (a toxic substance) builds up in the blood stream. This results in mental confusion.[21]

When an overdose occurs, the brain becomes overly depressed, causing the cerebral cortex to become less capable of doing its job. This makes the user feel lethargic, lifeless, and sluggish. Not only do tranquilizers depress the cerebral cortex, they also sedate (deaden) this important part of the brain. This causes it to be unable to sense what is happening around it, making the user feel overly calm and sleepy. This explains the tendency of the tranquilizer abuser to "nod off" or go to sleep when he or she should be doing something important—like driving a car in heavy traffic. Even when the abuser does not nod off, extreme fatigue and listlessness are still experienced. Often users will be too tired to do even the simplest tasks. All too frequently, the user simply "passes out" (goes into a drug-induced coma). This can have fatal consequences.[22]

# Questions for Discussion

1. What do you think are the appropriate uses for tranquilizers? What are the problems for which tranquilizers would be prescribed?

2. Why do you think so many people who are prescribed these medications eventually get addicted to them?

3. Why do you think so many people overdose on tranquilizers?

# 4

# One Teen's Story

This chapter, as the title suggests, is about one teen's experience with tranquilizers. The teen is Rob Roddy. The author has known him and his family for about ten years.

Like most tranquilizer users, Rob is also a polydrug abuser (someone who abuses several drugs). Very few drug abusers ever stick strictly to one drug. They experiment with several before settling on a drug of choice. Most continue to use one or more drugs, often at the same time. Teens who abuse tranquilizers usually do so in combination with other depressants, especially alcohol. This has led some drug abuse authorities, such as Dr. David Olms, to propose a new term that encompasses this concept. The term coined by Dr. Olms is "sedativism."[1]

Of all the drugs Rob Roddy tried, tranquilizers have had the most devastating impact. This is not surprising since tranquilizers greatly enhance the impact of other depressants. The author conducted the following interview with Roddy during December 1995.

His story is included here in much the same form in which he told it. The author has left his questions out because he wants the reader to have as much of a direct experience of Roddy's story as possible.[2]

## Rob Roddy's Story

You might be wondering just why I would want to tell the whole world about my life and my use of alcohol and drugs, especially tranquilizers. I mean, most people want to keep this kind of stuff secret, don't they? Well, not me. I want to share my story with as many people as humanly possible. My greatest hope is that by reading it, some of you might be convinced to decide against experimenting with these dangerous chemicals. Perhaps others of you might see where your drug abuse is leading you and what could happen to your life while there is still time for you to get help. If my story helps even one of you make such a decision, I will be very happy.

I had a great family as I was growing up. My father was a minister and a college professor. He was a kind and loving man, and he still is. My mother . . . did her best to raise me right and to teach me how to live. She, like my father, is also loving and kind. My older brother was and is a great guy. He tried his very best to be there for me. He was always willing to try to help me

Rob Roddy came from a model family. He had caring parents and a great big brother, but he started drinking and using drugs in the sixth grade.

with my problems. In many ways, I guess you could say I had as good a family as you can get in this world.

But something went terribly wrong in my life. I started experimenting with alcohol and drugs. At first it was just fun. I was just doing what everyone else seemed to be doing. No, I guess that's not completely true. Some of my friends never got into drugs. As *I* did, they ceased being as close to me as they once were. My counselor says that is one of the first symptoms of drug abuse—you lose the friends you had and find new, drug-abusing friends to hang out with.

That's exactly what I did. As drug use became the focus of my life, I lost interest in people who were not using. I was more interested in hanging around with other people who messed around with alcohol and drugs. I guess you could say my old friends and I just didn't have as much in common any more. In the end, the drugs and alcohol took control of my life, and did their best to ruin it. As you will see, they came pretty darn close to getting that job done.

I was in the sixth grade when I drank my first beer. In the seventh grade, I started smoking marijuana and taking white crosses (a form of speed). I also started huffing (inhaling) gas until I passed out. I did that about twice a week.

In the eighth grade, I really got into tranquilizers. This got so bad that, at one point, I popped several maximum-strength Valium tablets and was literally out of it all day. From that point on, I was hooked. Tranquilizers became my drug of choice. They were all I wanted. Of course, I would still drink alcohol or use some other drug when I couldn't get tranquilizers.

In the summer of the year between the ninth and tenth grades, I really got into it. By then I was popping a few tranquilizers every day and getting really loaded every weekend. I was also smoking pot whenever I couldn't find tranquilizers. Pot never made me feel as good, but it was more available. During my junior and senior years, I was doing tranquilizers, smoking pot, and drinking a lot. By then, I was getting loaded during the week as well as on the weekends.

I don't want to give you the impression that all I did was drink and do drugs. Most people thought I was just a normal teenager. I had a guitar which I loved to play. I was a great golfer and even had a job at the a golf club. I went to church with my parents and brother. I had a steady girlfriend named Amanda. My very favorite non-drug activity was playing volleyball, and I was very good at it.

I graduated from high school in 1993. That summer I got a job at a youth camp and taught repelling. I didn't bother attending college the first semester. Instead, I partied a lot and worked. Mostly, I partied. Work was about earning enough money to keep buying tranquilizers.

When school began again after Christmas, I enrolled and started attending the Bible college where my father taught. Out of my deep respect for him, I quit using all chemicals for two months. But I couldn't stay straight. The pull of tranquilizers was just too strong. When I started using again, I dropped out of the Bible college and started taking courses at a state university.

During that semester, two of my best drug-using friends were killed. They had been drinking and popping tranquilizers at one bar and decided to drive to another bar to continue the party. They were traveling down the interstate at a high rate of speed when they hit a parked semi (a large truck and trailer). One of them was so badly mangled that they never really found him. He was just crushed under the dash.

That summer, I got my own place. That was a big mistake. With no one around to watch me, I got really loaded every night. I was doing a lot of beer, some pot, and of course, my favorite, tranquilizers. This went on for about three months.

On the night of July 26, 1994, I was at a party for a friend who was coming home from the Army. Someone at the party had traveled a lot and brought huge amounts of Mexican tranquilizers to pass around. Amanda was there, too, but I was having very little to do with her and a lot to do with getting loaded. She got tired of the whole scene and decided to leave. She tried to get me to go with her, but I refused saying, "I'll call you when I'm ready to leave. It won't be long. You'll see." I was really wasted on Xanax and Irish whiskey. But I went right on partying and kept putting off calling her. In the end, I simply blew her off. I never did call. About 3:00 A.M., a friend and I started talking about our buddies who had been killed when they hit the semi. I said if I had gotten killed, I'd want someone to write a song about me. We decided that was a good idea, so we got my guitar and left. We drove to the exact spot where our friends had been killed. We parked on the feeder road right beside the spot marked by two white crosses—the sight of their deaths. It's at mile marker 116. My friend and I walked through the ditch to the freeway. I don't remember very much of this, but I was hit by a car. The lady who hit me said my friend was standing in the middle of the highway and she swerved to miss him and hit me while traveling about 60 miles per hour. The impact knocked me into the middle of the highway. I only broke one bone in my leg, but the impact was so forceful that it severed my aorta [a large artery] from my heart.

At Southwest Medical Center, doctors worked feverishly to reconnect that artery by using a new method involving synthetic materials. When my parents arrived, the doctors told them that the chances of my survival weren't good. They said I only had about a 3 percent chance of making it through the surgery because they would have to clamp off my heart which had already suffered severe damage. Even if I survived, they said they didn't know how much brain damage had been done. They estimated as much as 95 percent of my brain could already be too severely damaged to survive. They also told my parents that I already appeared to be paralyzed due to lack of blood to my spinal column. That causes the death of nerve cells, which are the only cells in the body which can't reproduce themselves. Once they die, they are gone forever. It's simply too late.

I regained consciousness five days later. Everyone was thrilled that I could actually think, talk, and move my upper body. I don't recall a lot about those first few days, but I remember seeing Amanda sleeping on the floor by my bed.

Hoping for some further return of lower body function, the doctors and nurses pushed me to get into the rehabilitation hospital two weeks later. At that point, I couldn't get out of bed or dress myself—and when I finally did, it took forty-five minutes. I also couldn't use the toilet or shower. The nurses had to do everything for me.

I had scabs from head to toe. To aid in my recovery, they put me in water every day and rubbed the scabs off. This was to prevent scarring and infection. I was eventually able to sit in a wheelchair. But when they forced me to wheel it twenty yards, the pain was absolutely incredible. After all, I'd had my whole chest cut open.

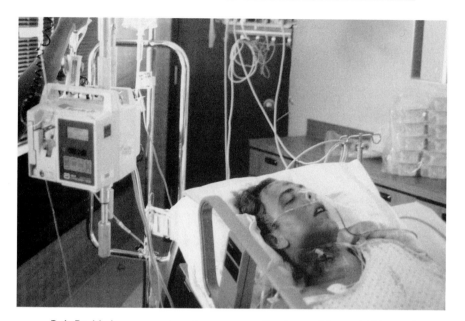

Rob Roddy lays unconcious in a room at Southwest Memorial Hospital after being hit by a car while wandering across a freeway. He was stoned on tranquilizers and alcohol at the time.

At one point, I got really sick with a high fever and had to be rushed back to the hospital. The doctors thought I had an infection in my aorta. After a week undergoing tests, they decided that I was ready to go back to rehab. The exact cause of my illness remains a mystery. No one ever found out what caused me to get so sick or to run such a high fever.

One of the things I remember about rehab is how many others were there because of being injured while under the influence of either tranquilizers or a combination of tranquilizers and alcohol. One guy was stoned and fell asleep on the railroad tracks. A train ran over him and severed his legs. Two people had broken their necks from diving into shallow water while they were loaded—one into a swimming pool, the other into a river. Another had rolled his truck while under the influence. Someone else was paralyzed from a car wreck because of using and driving. There were many others—too many others to mention.

During this time, I became addicted to morphine. I thought the stuff was cool, and I kept convincing the doctors to keep giving me more. Whenever they would cut it back I would complain that I was hurting bad. Eventually, they would give me more. Later, my counselor explained that all depressants are cross-addictive (That is, an addict can substitute one depressant for another). I was using morphine because I didn't have access to tranquilizers.

I remember at one point my mom got me a Dennis Byrd book. (Byrd was the New York Jets football player who broke his neck and was paralyzed for several months.) I overheard the doctor saying to my mom "I don't know if I'd give that to him. It might give him false hope." Then my mom came over to me and said "the doctors don't think you'll ever walk again." I was really bummed out about that and that night I began to pray, "I need you. I'm sorry. Please come back into my life." I gained a tremendous sense of peace at that time.

Two and a half months later, however, the doctors told me that they had done all they could. The paralysis in my legs was permanent. Too much of my spinal cord had died due to lack of blood. I left the rehab hospital in my wheelchair on October 26, 1994.

Three weeks later, Amanda and I broke up, although we're still friends. I spent the next two months waiting for the next semester to start. Then at a New Year's Eve party, I got wasted again. I popped a lot of Tylenol 3™ and tranquilizers, and I drank a lot of beer. This scared me so bad I went on the wagon again. But it didn't last. By April 1995, I was drinking and using tranquilizers heavily once again.

Then I got opportunities to talk to groups at churches and schools about what tranquilizer and alcohol abuse had done to me. I also talked to the kids at a summer camp. This caused me to do some serious reconsideration of my lifestyle, so I stopped popping tranquilizers and drinking.

Still, it was a tough period in my life. I was bored out of my skull most of the time. I couldn't drive yet because the driver's

Rob Roddy spends a lot of time talking to teenagers about the dangers of alcohol and other drugs. He is quick to say, "alcohol and tranquilizers are a deadly combination."

license people said I wasn't ready. I wanted to get into wheelchair sports, but I couldn't find others who were interested even though I made a hundred phone calls. I guess I just had too much idle time. So, I started using tranquilizers and drinking again.

This really did a trip on my head, so I quit witnessing to the schools and churches. I mean how could I witness to others when I was living such a lie? My whole life was a mess. I was spending most of my time loaded or looking for more tranquilizers. When I couldn't find them, I was so desperate I would try anything. I even got into "shrooms" (hallucinogenic mushrooms) for awhile.

On the positive side, I was finally allowed to drive and got a great car which was set up with hand controls. I loved this new freedom and once again swore off tranquilizers. I registered for college again in September 1995. But, before classes even started, I had gotten back into drinking and tranquilizers.

Later that month, a friend and I were coming from a party where we had consumed alcohol and used tranquilizers. My friend thought I was going to hit a parked car, so he grabbed the wheel and steered us away from it. Unfortunately, we skidded out of control for a tremendous distance, eventually hitting a house.

When the police arrived, I had to take a Breathalyzer™ (a test which is used to determine the amount of alcohol a person has used) because they thought I acted like I was drunk. Since I was more stoned on tranquilizers than I was on alcohol, I passed the test. But I knew the truth. I was miserable because I just couldn't quit using those darned pills.

In late October, I began seeing a drug and alcohol counselor for my addiction. With his help, I feel that I am finally making some progress in my life. I'm dating again, and doing a lot of the things I enjoy. I've gotten a racing wheelchair and I'm finally

What was left of Rob Roddy's new hand-controlled car after he got loaded on alcohol and tranquilizers and went for a drive with a friend. He lost control, went into a skid, and hit a house.

getting into wheelchair sports. I've even done some repelling recently. Yes, the wheelchair does cramp my style, but I'm determined to get on with my life.

Let me end my story by giving you some advice: If you haven't begun mixing tranquilizers and alcohol, don't start. If you've already started, quit. If you can't quit, get help.

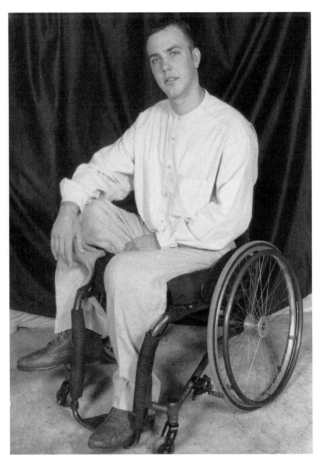

Rob Roddy as he is today, permanently paralyzed from the waist down. His message is simple, "Don't start using alcohol and drugs. If you've already started, quit. If you can't quit, get help!"

# Questions for Discussion

1. Why do you think no one noticed that Rob Roddy was having serious problems with drugs and alcohol?

2. Why were Rob Roddy's first attempts at treatment so unsuccessful?

3. If Rob Roddy was your friend and you knew how many drugs he was using and how much alcohol he was drinking, what would you have done?

# 5

# The Codependent Family

A codependent family is a family that has one or more addicted members. Understanding how codependent families function can be very difficult. In order to make it easier, discussion follows on the various relationships that these families engender (bring about). After that, several vignettes (small but true stories) from the lives of codependent families are included to illustrate these relationships.

These families react to the stress of having one or more addicted members in very specific ways.[1] This happens regardless of who the addicted family member is. It is also not dependent on how many family members are addicted. This has been observed and described by numerous people working in the

In addicted families, members are not allowed to ask certain questions. This addicted mother is about to slap her child because she asked about the hypodermic needle.

field of addiction and codependency. All of them agree that living in a codependent family is a painful existence and an emotionally devastating experience.

Even when actual drinking and drug use skip a generation, the pain and general dysfunction persist. Author Susan Thenephon says that it is passed on to grandchildren "without being diluted."[2] The overwhelming majority of professional alcohol and drug counselors agree.

Living in a family in which someone is addicted is an extremely stressful and very painful experience. The result is that members are pushed into one of several dysfunctional family roles.

The late Virginia Satir was the first major family theorist and researcher to discover this truth. She identified four such roles: the blamer—who blames someone else for the problem, the computer—who thinks but doesn't feel, the avoider—who distances from painful experiences, and the distractor—whose job it is to distract the family from their pain.[3]

Later, Sharon Wegscheider extended Satir's concepts and applied them to families in which one or more persons were addicted. She named and described six additional roles which were specific to codependent families. They are:

1. **The Dependent**—who is hooked on drugs.

2. **The Chief Enabler**—who makes excuses for the Dependent in an effort at protection, but whose efforts only result in protecting the Dependent from the consequences of addiction.

3. **The Hero**—usually a child who takes over as leader of the family.

4. **The Lost Child**—who finds being in the family so painful that he or she simply withdraws into his or her own world.

5. **The Mascot**—who distracts the family from its pain by being cute and wonderful.[4]

Salvador Minuchin, in his study of eating disorders, named two additional roles. They are:

1. **The Controlling Personality**—who controls everything about the other person.

2. **The Psychosomatic**—who responds by saying, "but you cannot control my body."[5]

Minuchin must take credit for being the first researcher to discover that dysfunctional roles only occur in relationship to one another. That is, each codependent family member is pushed into dysfunctional behavior by another family member's dysfunctional actions. This has become known as the "Theory of Reciprocity."

In much the same vein, this author studied codependent families and discovered several other reciprocal pairs. He described eight of these in a previous book.

1. **Clam-Grand Inquisitor Relationships**—in which one person "clams up" in response to another's "no win" questions.

2. **Incompetent Parent-Parentified Child Relationships**—in which the child takes over for a parent.

3. **Warrior-Peace Maker Relationships**—in which one family member is constantly smoothing the feathers ruffled by another.

4. **Hero-Rebel Relationships**—in which one family member balances the rebellion of another by becoming the family hero.

5. **Clown-Depressive Relationships**—in which one person has the job of taking everything seriously and another is in charge of lightening things up.

6. **Computer-Hysteric Relationships**—in which one person is in charge of thinking and the other is in charge of feeling.

7. **Mascot-Lost Child Relationships**—in which one person copes with stress by being in the spotlight while the other copes with it by "fading into the woodwork."

8. **Switchboard-Avoider Relationships**—in which one person avoids family members while another connects them.[6]

The remainder of this chapter will deal with five other relationships from the same study. They are the Crazy Maker-Psychotic relationships, Favored-Disfavored relationships, Discounter-Harlequin relationships, Messiah-Helpless relationships, and Gotcha-Paranoid relationships.

## Crazy Maker-Psychotic Relationships

This kind of a relationship happens when one family member suspects that a second family member is acting in a certain way, then accuses that person of the behavior. The person denies the behavior, but continues to do it. The following vignette illustrates this relationship.

Arnold and Cindy had been married for about six years when Cindy found herself attracted to a man where she worked. His name was Jerold. Soon Cindy and Jerold were having long lunches and working late together.

Arnold noticed a change in his and Cindy's level of intimacy and began to suspect that Cindy was interested in someone else, so he asked her about it. She responded that there was no one else in the whole world that she was interested in. This answer did not satisfy Arnold, but he wanted to believe her. Even so, he found that he just kept asking questions about it.

Soon Jerold invited Cindy to accompany him on a company trip. She accepted but was afraid to tell Arnold the truth, so she said that her boss had told her that she had to go to a distant city for a training workshop. Suspicious, Arnold asked if he could accompany her. Cindy replied that the other employees would think that was weird. Arnold spent the week obsessed with the fear that his wife was having an affair. When she returned, he questioned her for hours about everything that had happened on the trip.

The following week, she and Jerold (who actually had not had an affair with each other) laughed about Arnold's suspiciousness. They were just good friends.

In this case study, it is easy to see how Cindy's lack of honesty contributed to Arnold's lack of trust. What is not so easy to see is how Arnold's lack of trust contributed to Cindy's lack of honesty.

Suppose Cindy was attracted or addicted to tranquilizers and Arnold was suspicious about it. If Cindy lied about it, it would be the same set of interactions. That is, in fact, exactly what the situation was.

Along with her infatuaton with Jerold, Cindy had a long-term infatuation with Xanax. She had been abusing Xanax for about a year. Although her physician had told her not to increase her usage beyond four milligrams a day, she was using about twenty-five milligrams every day. She found that it was easy to get the drugs from doctors. All she had to do was to ask.

She also had to find enough doctors. By the time she had befriended Jerold, she had found seven. Each was prescribing Xanax and each was unaware that she had any other prescriptions.

Arnold could not figure out where all their money was going. When he asked Cindy, she just said that groceries were more expensive these days. Arnold was now convinced that Cindy had a boyfriend and that she was spending his hard earned money on him. This, of course, made him feel terrible.

One morning he walked into the kitchen and overheard Cindy talking on the telephone. "I told you never to call me here," she said.

"That does it!" Arnold shouted. "I want a divorce!"

"A divorce?" she asked. "Why?"

"Because I won't live with someone who's messing around on me," he said. "That's why."

"But . . . I'm . . . not," she stammered. "I don't want a divorce."

"Then explain where our money is going," he said, "and I don't want to hear anything about how expensive the groceries are!"

Trapped and afraid that she would lose her husband, Cindy blurted out the whole story.

Incidentally, the phone call was from a nurse at one of her doctors' offices calling to remind Cindy of her appointment the following day.

Dene Stamas, who teaches at the Alfred Adler Institute in Chicago, says that the problems she sees most in codependent families are mind reading, poor self-esteem, and resentment.[7] It is easy to see that there was plenty of each in this vignette. Cindy's behavior and denial made Arnold engage in mind reading, Arnold suffered from resentment, and both suffered from poor self-esteem.

## Discounter-Harlequin Relationships

In these relationships, one person is continually discounting another person's feelings, beliefs, and behavior. The other person responds by trying to feel, believe, or act differently. This results in the second person losing touch with who he or she is. They both become harlequins (a harlequin is a mask in which half the face is happy and half is sad.) People who are Harlequins may smile when they are unhappy or act friendly when they are angry. This relationship is exemplified by the following vignette.

Fourteen-year-old Suzie and her father had lived alone since her mother passed away. Her father was a minister and was a very devout man. When her mother died, he simply said, "It is God's will, do not be sad."

Suzie had done her best. All through the funeral, she had continued to greet friends and relatives with a smile. They all said that she was doing great. But she did not feel great—she felt terrible. She could not sleep and she had no appetite at all. But she never complained. She just could not let her father down. She simply had to be happy for him.

Her father kept right on working. In fact, the very day of the funeral he went to the church to work on his sermon for the following Sunday. He also continued to be his usual outgoing and friendly self, although sometimes at night Suzie thought she heard him crying.

Suzie soon found that she was afraid when she was not with her father. So, she started going to the church right after school. When he asked why, she simply said that she just wanted to be near him. He criticized her for this, saying, "A girl your age should be hanging around with her friends."

That summer, he sent Suzie to the country to spend a few weeks with her grandmother who was surprised at how thin Suzie had become. "You're just too nervous, Suzie" she said. "You need something to help you calm down."

So, she gave her one of her Valium tablets. For the first time since her mother's death Suzie felt at peace. Soon she was using several tablets a day. By the time her visit was over, Suzie had her own prescription—written by her grandmother's doctor.

Back at home things were still the same. She missed her mother terribly and she longed to be with her father. The problem was that he worked almost all the time. Before long Suzie had used up her prescription.

At that point, she started buying them on the street. Whenever she was out of money, she would just take some out of her father's wallet after he had fallen asleep at night.

He soon found out what was happening and confronted Suzie about the missing money. She said that several of her

With the mother now passed out from injecting Valium while drinking alcohol, her daughter's curiosity gets the best of her. She is about to sample her mother's whiskey.

friends were poor and did not have anything to eat for lunch. She claimed that she was buying these friends lunch every day.

But now her father was suspicious. She had to find another way to get her tranquilizers. Soon, she was "strawberrying" (trading sex for drugs). This worked until she got pregnant.

When she told her father that she was pregnant, he called her a slut and said he was ashamed of her. Then, he sent her to live with her grandmother.

This is typical of codependent relationships. Suzie's father never understood that he played a part in her problem. She never guessed that he was terrified of raising a child by himself.

Psychologist Mary Stewart and consultant Lynnzy Orr speak of the numerous and damaging rules in codependent families. These include the rule of control, the rule of secrecy, the rule of denial, and the rule of repression (hiding your true feelings). It is clear that all of these rules were at work in this family.[8] Suzie's father tried to control how she felt and how she acted. They both hid their true feelings from each other. Suzie and her father were both addicted: he to work and she to tranquilizers. Neither owned his or her own addictions. This is called "denial." Remember, the worst lies are always the ones we tell ourselves.

## Favored-Disfavored Relationships

Being in this kind of a relationship can be extremely painful, especially for the person who is disfavored. It occurs when one person (usually a child) has some characteristic that reminds someone (usually one of the parents) of someone they either do not like or someone they have an unresolved power struggle with (usually the other parent).

That characteristic can be something as simple as maleness or as complex as a speech pattern. Whatever it is, the disfavored one will then become the focus of intense but often subtle ridicule and rejection.

What makes this even more interesting is that the second parent will usually do the same thing to another child who may resemble the first parent in some way. This type of relationship can be seen in the following vignette.

Jose was the only person in his family who was as dark as his father, Arturo. He liked the fact that he took after him. He hoped that he would he as good of an athlete as well. His father played semiprofessional baseball with the Oklahoma City 89ers.

His brother, Juan, took after their mother, Betty. She had such a light complexion that his father called her his "gringa." He called Juan his "gringo." Their life together seemed ideal. At least, until Arturo injured his knee. It happened in the next to the last game of the season. Arturo was on third base when the opposing pitcher threw a wild pitch. As the catcher scrambled around looking for it, the third base coach shouted, "Steal home plate," and Arturo was running as fast as he could for home plate.

In the meantime, the catcher had located the ball and had turned and was also running toward home plate. Arturo knew it would be close and his only chance was to slide. Down he went. At the same moment, the catcher dived for the plate. There was a tremendous collision. "Safe!" shouted the umpire.

Jose was on his feet cheering his father's fantastic steal. He was so proud of his father, but soon his joy turned to concern.

The catcher had gotten up, but Arturo had not. He was lying there rolling back and forth holding his leg. He left the field on a stretcher.

At the hospital, the doctor gave Arturo and his family bad news. The injury was the kind that would require surgery. Afterward, it would take a lot of rehabilitation training. Only time would tell if Arturo would be able to play again.

Surgery went well, but Arturo was in tremendous pain. The doctor was giving him a painkiller that he became addicted to. So, the doctor took him off that drug and put him on a tranquilizer. Arturo became addicted to that drug as well. Soon he was more interested in staying loaded than he was in getting well.

Arturo's being around the house started getting on Betty's nerves. He was always there and, worse, he expected her to wait on him. Soon, a power struggle developed. Betty was tired of waiting on everyone. She wanted a life of her own. They needed money. So, Betty got a job. In response to this, Arturo became even more demanding.

This made Betty angry and resentful. She wanted Arturo to do his share. Instead, he did very little while she was working. He considered it beneath him. He believed cleaning house and cooking was a woman's job. His attitude made Betty even angrier.

One day, Jose asked his mother to get him a glass of milk. "Get it yourself," she said. "You're just like that father of yours. You expect everyone to wait on you. Well, forget it. I am not your slave!"

"Hey," said Arturo motioning toward Juan, "He's not like your little sissy Gringo. Jose is a man."

That is how it started. However, it got much worse. One of today's most well-known and insightful family researchers and therapists, Dr. Michael Nichols, refers to this as a cross-generational alliance.[9] It happens when at least one of the parents joins with a child against the other parent. In this way, the marital relationship is compromised. This is typical of codependent families.

## Messiah-Helpless Relationships

This relationship happens when one person is absolutely unable to help himself or herself. The debilitating factor can be anything from joblessness to being addicted to drugs. The "messiah" then saves the helpless one because of his or her great, but unmerited, love.

Please note that it is essential for the love to be unmerited (unearned). If the helpless one were to get a job or stop using drugs—the contract upon which their relationship is based would be broken. This vignette shows this predicament.

Joan had been addicted to tranquilizers for ten years. She had tried to stop several times, but she always went back to using again. Her longest period of sobriety was twenty-seven days.

She was not able to hold a job, either. She had twelve jobs in the last four years. The same thing happened each time. Either her employer would figure out that she was an addict because of her constant nodding off, or she would get caught sleeping on the job. A few times, she caused on-the-job accidents because she was loaded. Once, when she was working in a butcher shop, she almost cut her finger off in a meat slicer. All of her jobs ended the same way; she was asked to leave.

Then she met John. He was bright, well-read, and handsome. He had a master's degree in business and a great job. He even owned his own home. Best of all, he fell in love with Joan the moment he laid eyes on her.

He met her at pool party in San Diego. She was sitting on the side of the pool with her legs in the water. Her long blond hair was pulled back in a ponytail. Of course, she was loaded—which made her happy and she giggled as she moved her feet back and forth in the water.

John could not believe his eyes; he thought she was the prettiest woman he had ever seen. So, he walked over and sat down beside her. She laughed at his jokes and told him how witty he was. He asked for her phone number and the rest was history. She lost another job that next week and she was evicted from her apartment a month later.

John came to her rescue. First, he was going to pay her rent. Then he offered to let her move in with him. When she told him about her tranquilizer use, he said it was no big deal. His mother had been a heroin addict and had died from an overdose when he was thirteen. Compared to that, tranquilizers were nothing, he said. If anything, it just made him want to take care of her even more. After living together for two weeks, they got married.

John was more than happy to keep her supplied with tranquilizers, just so long as she was there when he got home and she was faithful to him. Other than that, she could do as she wanted. It was after she had wrecked his forth BMW, that John started to worry. But he never once complained. As long as she needed him, he knew she would stay.

The real problem, from John's perspective, started when Joan started talking about getting treatment and going to college. His response was, "What's the matter, don't I take good care of you?" When she finally did admit herself to a chemical dependency treatment center, John brought her one of her bottles of tranquilizers when he visited.

This kind of relationship is typical in the codependent family. Robert Ackerman, noted author, professor, and founder of the National Association of Children of Alcoholics, has found that adult children from codependent families still suffer from the damage done in their families. This expresses itself by causing these people to react in dysfunctional ways. Among those dysfunctional interactions are those who become hyper-mature and those who adopt a passive and helpless orientation to life.[10]

## Gotcha-Paranoid Relationships

In this type of relationship, one person is continually waiting for the other person to make a mistake. When the first person does, the second responds by attacking with an almost sadistic glee. One way or another he or she says, "Gotcha!" (got you).

The other person responds to this by becoming more on guard. This, of course, only makes it more of a certainty that he or she will mess up, since he or she is driven to distraction by worrying about messing up. This type of relationship is depicted in the following vignette.

Keith was an unusually hard worker. He opened the family service station every morning before breakfast and worked there until his father relieved him so he could eat. After breakfast, he helped his mother do the dishes. Then, he went to school. When he came home, he worked at the service station until supper time. After supper, he did his homework.

When he got to the service station after school one evening, his mother and father were both there. "Grandma died today," his mother said. That evening they drove to New Jersey, to be with the rest of the family and to make preparations for the funeral.

Keith had been close to his grandfather in the past, but they had not seen each other for over a year. After the funeral, many neighbors and friends came to the house with food and stayed to eat it with the family. When all the company was gone, there was a huge stack of dirty dishes, so Keith started trying to help by washing as many as he could.

His grandfather was by his side every minute. "Be careful!" he would say, "that belonged to your grandmother." By the time the dishes were done, Keith had broken two plates and a glass, and he was a nervous wreck.

The next day, it was decided that Grandpa would come to live with Keith's family. Keith was not so sure that was a good idea, but he convinced himself that grandpa was just reacting to the loss of his wife. He would get better with time, Keith reasoned. Unfortunately, things did not get better after they returned home. Grandpa was always at the service station and he was constantly critical of Keith. This got so bad that Keith hated going to work and his hands shook all the time.

Finally, the family doctor noticed that Keith seemed to be under a good deal of stress. She asked Keith what was going on, and he told her the whole story. He left her office with a prescription for Valium.

When grandpa found out about it, he hit the roof. "People who use drugs are weak," he said.

This is consistent with codependent family functioning. They often lose their ability to self-correct. This is especially true when one member is overly critical.[11]

# Questions for Discussion

1. After reading this chapter, what do you think is the most damaging thing about living in a codependent family?

2. Who do you think suffers the most severe damage in codependent families?

3. Do you recognize any of these dysfunctional family relationships? If so, what do you think should be done about it?

# 6

# Getting Help

If you or someone you know is addicted to tranquilizers and you or they want help, this chapter is written just for you. Read on. Usually, the best place to start looking for help is right where you live—with your parents! Most parents really do care about their children and want to help. They may be shocked, angry, and confused when you first tell them, but they usually will get over that and try their best to help you.[1] However, if your parents are also addicted, you may want to look elsewhere for help.

If, for whatever reason, you feel you cannot talk to your parents about a drug problem, you can always go to your school counselor. He or she probably knows quite a bit about substance abuse and addiction and should be prepared to help you.[2]

Another option is to speak to your minister, priest, or rabbi. These spiritual leaders probably went into the clergy because they wanted to help. It is what most of them do best. Just give them a call or ask to speak to them in person. In addition, many members of the clergy have had specialized training in chemical dependency counseling.[3]

Relatives other than your parents can also be helpful. If you have a special relationship with a grandfather or grandmother, he or she might be just the person you need to talk with. Do not forget about your other relatives including aunts, uncles, older brothers or sisters, or cousins. Just be open and honest and let them help. Be sure to tell them what you have learned about addiction. You might even let them read this book.[4]

Do not forget about your family doctor. He or she could do a lot to help. Doctors are trained to know exactly how to handle a situation like this. They are especially well trained to know what to do if there is a danger of you or your friend needing special medical help. Your doctor can especially help with complications from an overdose or withdrawal.[5]

If you are trying to find help for someone other than yourself who is addicted, you may or may not want to discuss the issue with that person. Surprised? Well, hang on. We will take a closer look at this. Say you have a friend who you think is in big trouble with drugs. Is your friend the kind of person you can talk to about this problem? Are you likely to get your friend extremely angry if you mention it? What would happen if you told his or her parents?

One of the best ways of getting help is to call one of the alcohol or drug treatment professionals. They are the professionals who are trained and certified to deal with alcohol and drug problems. They are called Certified Alcohol and Drug Counselors (CADC), Master Addiction Counselors (MAC), or International Certified Alcohol and Drug Counselors (ICADC). You can find one in most Yellow Pages under the heading of "alcohol and drug counselors." If for some reason this does not work, you can always call your state, province, or territory substance abuse agency. (See the list following this chapter.)

While money to pay for service can be an issue, you do not need to worry about whether you have the funds before you call a CADC, MAC, or ICADC. That is something you can discuss on the phone. In some agencies these professionals are paid by the state, so their services are free. If the alcohol and drug professional you call cannot take free clients and you cannot afford to pay, he or she is ethically bound to refer you to someone who can help you. Remember, if you are the person who has the problem with tranquilizers, your parent's health insurance may pay the costs associated with treatment services.

If you are the person who is addicted, you will have to tell your parents at some point. A CADC, MAC, or ICADC should be able to help with that. They are used to breaking the news to parents. Sure your parents will probably have a hard time with it, but they will want you to get help. The bottom line is, if you are addicted, you need treatment. All other considerations must be put on hold until that happens. The important thing is to get help for your addiction.

If the person you want to help is one or both of your parents, do you think they would be cooperative? About half of them will be. The other half will not. Some of them will get very angry at you for even making the suggestion that they have a drug problem and could use some help. If this is the case, there are still ways for you to be instrumental in getting them the help they so desperately need.(See "Intervention" below.)

If your parent is the kind of person who will listen to you, it might be best to start talking about what you have experienced and what your feelings are about his or her using drugs and/or drinking. Talk about how his or her mood changes and whether or not you have been embarrassed around him or her. Discuss your reluctance to invite friends to your home because of not knowing in what condition you will find your parent.

Then, ask him or her to get help. This is important because one of the ways that an addict deceives himself or herself is that he or she thinks the problem can be handled alone. If this were true, he or she would have quit years ago. Be sure to ask him or her to talk to a CADC, MAC, or ICADC about their problem with drugs.

If your parent will not get help on his or her own, you may have to call the drug professional yourself. If this becomes necessary, you will need to have a counselor who knows how to use a technique called an "intervention." For your information, the actual process of doing an intervention is described below.

## Intervention

An intervention is a method for breaking through an addict's denial system. All addicts have difficulty admitting to themselves and others that they have a problem with alcohol or drugs. The intervention helps them see what is happening to them through the eyes of other people.[6]

If the drug professional sets up an intervention, you will be asked to make a list of all the people who have been around the addict when he or she was under the influence. As you may guess, this could be a very long list. Then, you will be asked to make your best guess about which ones would be willing to help. Once this is done, the counselor will call and invite each of them to a meeting.

At that meeting, the counselor will ask each person to keep everything that happens confidential. Those who can not promise to do so will be thanked for coming and asked to leave. At that point, the drug professional will explain the purpose of an intervention and describe how it works. Part of that description will be "a loving confrontation designed to break through the addict's denial system."

This means that each person will be asked to make a list of the times that he or she experienced the addict under the influence and how he or she felt at the time. Each person will also be asked to state in a kind and loving way what he or she needs from the addict in the future. This is basically practice for the actual intervention.

When the day comes, the addict will be invited to the meeting. He or she will not know that all of the other people are waiting. When the addict arrives, the drug professional will get the addict to agree to be silent until everyone else has had a chance to speak. At that point, each person will speak to the addict using the skills he or she has learned.

An example would be for the addict's employer to say, "Joe, you've been a good employee over the years. But your drinking has hurt the company. At last year's Christmas party you were stoned, and you kept telling Mrs. Pierce all those dirty jokes. Then you left and got a drunk driving ticket in the company car. Mrs. Pierce is not only one of our best customers, she is president

One of the members of the Lawton-Fort Still Moonlight Walk Against Drugs is shown here. Members walk to show support for organizations that have pledged to fight drug abuse in their community.

of the local MADD (Mothers Against Drunk Driving) organization. Her daughter was killed by a drunk driver. She saw you get arrested. Joe, I care about you and about your family, but if you don't get treatment, I'll have to fire you. I'm asking you to go to treatment."

Another example would be for "Joe's" brother to say, "Joe, you know I've always been there for you, but your drug use has hurt our relationship. Last weekend, the way you behaved in front of my wife and children was uncalled for. You were so loaded when you came back from that hunting trip that you forgot the shotgun was loaded. You accidentally shot it off in the front yard and shot down one of our trees. Then, you laughed about it! My family was terrified. So was I. You could have hit any one of us. Joe, I love you, but if you don't get treatment, you can't come to my house any more. I'm begging you to get help. Please, Joe!"

Joe's wife might say, "Joe, I've loved you desperately for twenty years. During that time, I've never had eyes for anyone but you. You've been more than a husband; you've been my best friend, my lover, my sweetheart, my life. But the drugs and booze have changed you, Joe. Two weeks ago, you came home so loaded that you could hardly walk. On the way to the bedroom, you fell down the stairs. When I tried to help you get up, you began cursing at me in front of the kids. Then you hit me, Joe. I still love you, but if you don't get help, I can't live with you any more. It's treatment or a divorce, Joe. Please choose treatment." When interventions are done well, about 90 percent of addicts go to treatment. But, it is vitally important that the intervention is done right. Do not try to do an intervention by yourself. Call a drug treatment professional who is trained to do interventions.

A member of "Students Against Drunk Driving" (SADD) is shown here. SADD members are very active in getting help for friends so that they will not drive drunk.

You do not want to blow this. For many addicts, an intervention is their last chance. Remember, untreated addiction can be fatal.

## Treatment Options

There are several kinds of treatment. Outpatient treatment usually consists of weekly counseling sessions. This is usually an option for those who are not severely addicted.

Addicts who have been addicted for a long time will need inpatient treatment. This will take place in a treatment center. The addict will actually live there for thirty days or longer. If the addict is addicted to alcohol, tranquilizers, or barbiturates, he or she will to go to a treatment center that is also a part of a hospital. This is so the addict will have the services of a medical detox center. This is necessary because these drugs are very dangerous to stop using after a period of abuse. It is best to do so under a doctor's care.

In any case, treatment is what will return your life and those of your family members to normal. Actually, it could be much better than normal, it could be fantastic.

# Questions for Discussion

1. If you had a friend you thought was addicted, would you discuss it with him or her?

2. If you needed to ask for help for an addictive problem, who would be your first choice to ask? Your second choice? Your third? Explain your choices.

3. Who would be the hardest person in your life to tell that you were addicted? Why? What would help?

# Where to Write

## State, Province, and Territorial Authorities

### Alabama Department of Mental Health
### Division of Substance Abuse Services
200 Interstate Park Drive
Montgomery, AL 36193
(334) 242-3417

### Alaska Department of Health and Social Services
### Division of Alcoholism and Drug Abuse
PO Box 110607
Juneau, AK 99811-0607
(907) 465-2071

### Government of American Samoa
### Social Service Division
Alcohol and Drug Program
Pago Pago, AS 96799
(684) 633-4606

### Arizona Department of Health Services
### Division of Behavioral Health Services
Office of Substance Abuse
2122 East Hiland
Phoenix, AZ 85016
(602) 381-8996

### Arkansas Bureau of Alcohol
### and Drug Prevention
108 East Seventh Street
400 Waldon Building
Little Rock, AR 72201
(501) 280-4501

## California Executive Office Governor's Council on Drug and Alcohol Abuse
1700 K Street, Fifth Floor,
Sacramento, CA 95814-4037
(916) 445-1943

## Colorado Department of Health Alcohol and Drug Abuse Division
4300 Cherry Creek Drive, South
Denver, CO 80222-1530
(303) 692-2930

## Connecticut Department of Public Health and Addiction Services
999 Asylum Avenue, Third Floor
Hartford, CT 06105
(203) 418-6832

## Delaware Division of Alcoholism, Drug Abuse, and Mental Health
1901 North Dupont Highway
Newcastle, DE 19720
(302) 577-4461

## District of Columbia Alcohol and Drug Abuse Services
1300 First Street, North East
Suite 325
Washington, DC 20002
(202) 727-1762

## Federated States of Micronesia Department of Human Services
Post Office Box PS70
Palikir, Pohnpie, FM 96941
(691) 320-2643

## Florida Department of Health and Rehabilitative Services
1317 Winewood Boulevard
Building 6, Room 183
Tallahassee, FL 32301
(904) 488-0900

## Georgia Department of Alcohol and Drug Services
Two Peachtree Street NE, Fourth Floor
Atlanta, GA 30309
(404) 851-8961

## Guam Department of Mental Health and Substance Abuse
PO Box 9400
Tamuning, GU 96911
(671) 646-9262-69

## Hawaii Department of Health Alcohol and Drug Abuse Division
PO Box 3378
Honolulu, HI 96801
(808) 586-3962

## Idaho Department of Mental Health Division of Family and Children Services
405 West State Street, Third floor
Boise, ID 83702
(208) 334-0800

## Illinois Department of Alcoholism and Substance Abuse
22 South College Avenue, Third Floor
Springfield, IL 62704
(217) 785-9067

## Indiana Division of Mental Health
W-353, 402 West Washington Street
Indianapolis, IN 46204-2739
(317) 232-7816

## Iowa Department of Public Health Division of Substance Abuse
Lucas State Office Building, Third Floor
Des Moines, IA 50319
(515) 281-4417

## Kansas Alcohol and Drug Services
Biddle Building, 300 Southwest Oakley
Topeka, KS 66606-1861
(913) 296-3925

**Kentucky Department of Mental Health Division of Substance Abuse**
275 East Main Street
Frankfort, KY 40621
(502) 564-2880

**Louisiana Department of Health and Hospital Office of Alcohol and Drug Abuse**
1201 Capitol Access Road
Baton Rouge, LA 70821-2790
(504) 342-6717

**Maine Office of Substance Abuse**
State House Station #159
24 Stone Street
Augusta, ME 04333-1519
(207) 287-2595

**Maryland State Alcohol and Drug Abuse Administration**
201 West Preseton Street
Baltimore, MD 21201
(410) 225-6925

**Massachusetts Division of Substance Abuse Services**
150 Tremont Street
Boston, MA 02111
(617) 624-5111

**Michigan Department of Public Health Center for Substance Abuse Services**
3423 North Logan/Martin Luther King, Jr., Boulevard
Lansing, MI 48909
(517) 335-8808

**Minnesota Department of Human Services Chemical Dependency Program Division**
444 Lafayette Road
St. Paul, MN 55155-3823
(612) 296-4610

**Mississippi Department of Mental Health Division of Alcohol and Drug Abuse**
Robert E. Lee Office Building, Eleventh Floor
Jackson, MS 39201
(601) 359-1288

**Missouri Department of Health Division of Alcohol and Drug Abuse**
1706 East Elm Street
Jefferson City, MO 65109
(573) 751-4942

**Montana Department of Corrections and Human Services Alcohol and Drug Abuse Division**
539 Eleventh Avenue
Helena, MT 59601-1301
(406) 444-2827

**Nebraska Department of Public Institutions Division of Alcoholism and Drug Abuse**
PO Box 94728
Lincoln, NE 68509-4728
(402) 471-2851 Ext. 5583

**Nevada Department of Human Resources Bureau of Alcohol and Drug Abuse**
505 East King Street, Room 500
Carson City, NV 89710
(702) 687-4790

**New Hampshire Office of Alcohol and Drug Abuse Prevention**
105 Pleasant Street
Concord, NH 03301
(603) 271-6119

**New Jersey Department of Health Division of Alcoholism, Drug Abuse and Addiction Services**
CN 362
Trenton, NJ 08625-0362
(609) 292-5760

**New Mexico Department of Health Behavioral Health Services Division/SA**
1190 Saint Francis Drive,
Room 3200 North
Santa Fe, NM 87501
(505) 827-2601

**New York Office of Alcoholism and Substance Abuse Services**
Executive Park South
PO Box 8200
Albany, NY 12203
(518) 457-2061

**North Carolina Division of Mental Health Developmental Disabilities and Substance Abuse Services**
325 North Salisbury Street
Raleigh, NC 27611
(919) 733-4670

**North Dakota Department of Human Services Division of Alcoholism and Drug Abuse**
1829 East Capitol Avenue
Bismark, ND 58501
(701) 328-2310

**Ohio Department of Alcohol and Drug Addiction Services**
Two Nationwide Plaza, 12th Floor
280 North High Street
Columbus, OH 43215-2537
(614) 466-3445

**Oklahoma Department of Mental Health and Substance Abuse Services**
PO Box 53277
Capitol Station
Oklahoma City, OK 73152-3277
(405) 522-3908

## Oregon Department of Human Resources
## Office of Alcohol and Drug Abuse Programs
1178 Chemeketa Street, Northeast
Room 102
Salem, OR 97310
(503) 371-2810

## Pennsylvania Department of Health
## Office of Drug and Alcohol Programs
PO Box 90
Harrisburg, PA 17108
(717) 787-9857

## Puerto Rico Department of Anti-Addiction Services
Box 21414, Ro Piedras Station
Rio Piedras, PR 00928-1414
(809) 764-3796

## Rhode Island Office of Substance Abuse
PO Box 20363
Cranston, RI 02920
(401) 464-2091

## South Carolina Commission
## on Alcohol and Drug Abuse
3700 Forest Drive
Columbia, SC 29204
(803) 734-9520

## South Dakota Department of Human Services
## Division of Alcohol and Drug Abuse
Hillsview Plaza, East Highway 34
Pierre, SD 57501-5090
(605) 773-3123

## Tennessee Department of Health
## Bureau of Alcohol and Drug Abuse Services
Cordell Hull Building, Room 255
Nashville, TN 37247-4401
(615) 741-1921

**Texas Health Association**
6006 North Mesa, Suite 600
El Paso, TX 79912
(915) 581-6645

**Trust Territories/Pacific Islands**
**Office of the Governor**
Health Services
Sapan, MP 96950
011-670-2348950

**Utah Department of Social Services**
**Division of Substance Abuse**
PO Box 45500
Salt Lake City, UT 84404
(801)538-3939

**Vermont Office of Alcohol**
**and Drug Abuse Programs**
103 South Main Street
Waterbury, VT 05676
(802) 241-2170

**Virgin Islands Division of Mental Health,**
**Mental Retardation, and Substance Abuse Services**
Charles Harwood Memorial Hospital
Christianstead, St. Croix
U.S. Virgin Islands, 00820
(809) 773-1311 Ext. 3013

**Virginia Department of Mental health,**
**Mental Retardation and Substance Abuse Services**
Office of Substance Abuse Services
PO Box 1797
Richmond, VA 23214
(804)786-3906

**Washington Department of Social and Health Services**
**Division of Alcohol and Substance Abuse**
PO Box 45330
Olympia, WA 98504-5330
(360) 438-8200

**West Virginia Division of Alcoholism
and Drug Abuse**
1900 Kanawha Boulevard
Building Six, Room B-738
Charleston, WV 25305
(304) 558-2276

**Wisconsin Bureau of Substance Abuse Services**
PO Box 7851
Madison, WI 53707
(608) 266-2717

**Wyoming Division of Behavioral Health**
447 Hathaway Building
Cheyenne, WY 82002
(307) 777-7094

# Helpful Organizations

### ALA-NON AND ALA-TEEN HEADQUARTERS
PO Box 862, Midtown Station
New York, NY 10018-0862
(800) 344-2666

### ALCOHOLICS ANONYMOUS WORLD SERVICE, INC.
475 Riverside Drive
New York, NY 10115
(212) 870-3400

### AMERICAN COUNCIL FOR DRUG EDUCATION
204 Monroe Street
Rockville, MD 20852
(800) 488-DRUG

### CENTER FOR SUBSTANCE ABUSE
TREATMENT INFORMATION
11426-28 Rockville Pike, Suite 410
Rockville, MD 20852
(800) 662-HELP (English-speaking callers)
(800) 66-AYUDA (Spanish-speaking callers)

## CHILDREN OF ALCOHOLICS FOUNDATION, INC.
PO Box 4185, Grand Central Station
New York, NY 10115
(800) 359-2623
(212) 754-0656

## FAMILIES ANONYMOUS, INC.
PO Box 528
Van Nuys, CA 91408
(818) 989-7841

## INTERNATIONAL CERTIFICATION
## RECIPROCITY CONSORTIUM
3725 National Drive, Suite 213
Raleigh, NC 27612
(919) 781-9734

## MOTHERS AGAINST DRUNK DRIVING (MADD)
511 E. John Carpenter Freeway, No. 700
Irving, TX 75062
(214) 744-6233
(800) 438-6233

## NAR-ANON FAMILY GROUPS
Post Office Box 2562
Palos Verdes Peninsula, CA 90274
(310) 547-5800

## NATIONAL ASSOCIATION OF ALCOHOL
## AND DRUG ABUSE COUNSELORS
3717 Columbia Pike, Suite 300
Arlington, VA 2220
(800) 548-0497

## NATIONAL ASSOCIATION FOR
## CHILDREN OF ALCOHOLICS
11426 Rockville Pike, Suite 100
Rockville, MD 20852
(301) 468-0985

## NATIONAL BOARD FOR CERTIFIED COUNSELORS
3 Terrace Avenue, Suite D
Greensboro, NC 27403
(910) 547-0607

## NATIONAL CLEARINGHOUSE FOR ALCOHOL AND DRUG INFORMATION
PO Box 2345
Rockville, MD 20852-2345
(301) 468-2600
(800) 729-6686

## NATIONAL COUNCIL ON ALCOHOLISM AND DRUG DEPENDENCE
12 West 21st Street
New York, NY 10010
(212) 206-6770

## NATIONAL FAMILIES IN ACTION
2296 Henderson Mill Road, Suite 204
Atlanta, GA 30345
(404) 934-6364

## NATIONAL FEDERATION OF DRUG-FREE YOUTH
8730 Georgia Avenue
Silver Springs, MD 20910
(800) 554-5437

## STUDENTS AGAINST DRUNK DRIVING (SADD)
PO Box 800
Marlborough, MA 01752
(508) 481-3568

# National Hotlines

**DRUG AND ALCOHOL HOTLINE** (800) 252-6465
**NATIONAL INSTITUTE ON DRUG ABUSE** (800) 662-HELP
**THE COCAINE HOTLINE** (800) COCAINE

# Chapter Notes

## Chapter 1

1. *Depressants* (South Deerfield, Mass.: Channing L. Bette, 1990), p. 6.
2. Andrew Weil and Winifred Rosen, *Chocolate to Morphine* (Boston, Mass.: Houghton Miffin, 1993), p. 78.
3. Gail Winger, *Valium: The Tranquil Trap* (New York: Chelsea, 1988), p. 25; Regina Avraham, *The Downside of Drugs* (New York: Chelsea, 1988), p. 67; Richard Corliss, "His Own Private Agony," *Time*, November 15, 1993, p. 111.
4. "Jackson Admits Painkiller Addiction," *The Daily Oklahoman*, November 14, 1994, p. 1.; Avraham, p. 71.; Ibid., p. 70.
5. *Depressants*, p. 4.
6. Oakley Ray and Charles Ksir, *Drugs, Society, & Human Behavior* (St. Louis, Mo.: Times Mirror/Mosby, 1987), p. 139.
7. Ibid.
8. Ibid.
9. Robert O'Brien and Morris Chafetz, *The Encyclopedia of Alcoholism* (New York: Facts on File, 1982), pp. 214-215.
10. Kenneth Jones, Louis Shainberg, and Curtis Byer, *Drugs and Alcohol* (New York: Harper and Row, 1969), p. 92.
11. Hardin Jones and Helen Jones, *Sensual Drugs* (London, England: Cambridge University Press, 1978), p. 45.
12. Ibid., pp. 45-46.
13. Proverbs 23:29-35. *New English Bible* (London: Oxford University and Cambridge University, 1970), pp. 776-777.
14. O'Brien and Chafetz, p. 89.
15. Ibid.

16. Andrew Kowl, ed., "Opium," *High Times Encyclopedia of Recreational Drugs* (New York: Stonehill, 1978), p. 217.

17. Ibid., p. 214.

18. Melford Spiro, *Buddhism and Society* (New York: Harper & Row, 1970), p.45.

19. Jones, Shainberg, and Byer, p. 35.

20. "Morphine," *High Times Encyclopedia of Recreational Drugs*, p. 223.

21. Weil and Rosen, p. 16.

22. Ray and Ksir, p. 34.

23. Hardin and Helen Jones, p. 189.

24. Ray and Ksir, p. 254.

25. "Opium," *High Times Encyclopedia of Recreational Drugs*, p. 224.

26. Ibid., p. 225.

27. Helen and Hardin Jones, p. 190.

28. Ray and Ksir, p. 126.

29. "Sedative-Hypnotics," *High Times Encyclopedia of Recreational Drugs*, p. 242.

30. Ray and Ksir, p. 126.

31. "Sedative-Hypnotics," *High Times Encyclopedia of Recreational Drugs*, p. 242.

## Chapter 2

1. Andrew Weil and Winifred Rosen, *From Chocolate to Morphine* (Boston: Houghton Mifflin, 1993), pp. 73-74.

2. Ibid., p. 74.

3. Hardin Jones and Helen Jones, *Sensual Drugs* (London, England: Cambridge University Press, 1978), p. 100.

4. Elisabeth Stone, "Low Anxiety," *Mademoiselle*, January 1993, p. 46

5. "Sedative-Hypnotics," *High Times Encyclopedia of Recreational Drugs*, p. 242.

6. Stephen Apthorp, *Alcohol and Substance Abuse* (Winton, Conn.: Morehouse-Barlow), p. 74

7. Oakley Ray and Charles Ksir, *Drugs, Society, & Human Behavior* (St. Louis, Mo.: Times Mirror/Mosby, 1978), p. 129.

8. Apthorp, p. 76.

9. Weil and Rosen, p. 76.

10. Ray and Ksir, p. 28.

11. Mick Jagger and Keith Richards, "Rock On!", Vol. 2, *Illustrated Encyclopedia of Rock and Roll: The Modern Years, 1956 to Present,* Norm Nited, ed. (New York: Thomans Crowell, 1978), p. 404.

12. *Physicians' Desk Reference* (Montvale, N.J.: Medical Data Economic Production Company, 1995), p. 2078.

13. "Tranquilizers," *High Times Encyclopedia of Recreational Drugs*, p. 247.

14. "High Anxiety," *Consumer Reports*, January 1993, p. 23.

15. Ibid., p. 25.

16. "On Drugs and Therepeutics," *The Medical Newsletter* (New Rochelle, N.Y.: The Medical Letter, Inc., 1987), p. 86.

17. Stone, p. 48.

18. "High Anxiety," *Consumer Reports*, January 1993, p. 20.

19. Brian O'Reilly, "Drugmakers," *Fortune,* July 29, 1991, p. 63.

20. Cynthia Cotts, "The Pushers in the Suites," *The Nation,* August 31/September 7, 1992, p. 208.

21. "Treatment of Acute Drug Abuse Reactions," *The Medical Newsletter* (New Rochelle, N.Y.: The Medical Letter, Inc., 1987), p. 84.

22. "Controlled Substance Chart", *The 1995 Physician's Desk Reference* (Montvale N.J.: Medical Economics Data Production Company), p. 1112.

23. Lawrence Young, et. al., *Recreational Drugs* (New York: Macmillan, 1989), p. 220.

24. Anthorp, p. 73.

25. "Depressants," *Confusions About Alcohol and Other Drugs* (Jackson, Mich.: National Child Safety Council, 1991), p. 8.

26. Cotts, p. 210.

27. Ibid.

28. Regina Avraham, *The Downside of Drugs* (New York: Chelsea, 1988), pp. 68-71.

29. Ibid.

30. Ibid.

31. Cotts, p. 208.

32. "Developmental Patterns of the Use of Legal, Illegal and Medically Prescribed Drugs from Adolescence to Young Adulthood," *Etimology of Drug Abuse* (Rockville, Md.: U.S. National Institute on Drug Abuse, Department of Health and Human Services, 1987), p. 201.

## Chapter 3

1. Don Ladig, ed., "Diasepam," *Nursing Drug Reference* (St. Louis, Mo.: Mosby, 1993), pp. 314-315.

2. Suzanne Loebl and George Spratto, "Anxiety Agents," *The Nurse's Drug Handbook* (New York: John Wiley and Sons, 1986), p. 391.

3. Lillian Brunner and Doris Suddarth, eds., "Assessing Neurologic Function," *Medical-Surgical Nursing* (Philadelphia: The J. B. Lippincott Company, 1983 ), p. 366.

4. Ibid., p. 1395.

5. Ibid., p. 1399.

6. Hardin Jones and Helen Jones, *Sensual Drugs* (London, England: Cambridge University Press, 1978), p. 248.

7. Barbara Kozier and Glenora Erb, *Fundamentals of Nursing* (Menlo Park, Calif.: Addison-Wesley Publishing Company, 1987), p. 329.

8. Brunner and Suddarth, p. 1489.

9. Ibid., p. 1495.

10. Kosier and Erb, p. 1065.

11. Judith Haber, Anita McMahon, Pam Hoskins, and Barbara Sideleau, *Psychiatric Nursing* (St. Louis, Mo.: Mosby Publishing, 1985), p. 325.

12. Ellen Janosik and Janet Davies, *Psychiatric Mental Health Nursing* (Boston: Jones and Bartlett Publishing, 1986), p. 213.

13. Kosier and Erb, p. 1107.

14. Janosik and Davies, p. 213.
15. Kosier and Erb, p. 1118.
16. Oakley Ray and Charles Ksir, *Drugs, Society, and Human Behavior*, (St. Louis, Mo.: Times Mirror/Mosby, 1987), p. 135.
17. John Marks, *The Benzodiazapines: Use, Overuse, Misuse, Abuse* (Lancaster, England: MPT Press, 1978), p. 21.
18. Haber, McMahon, Hoskins, and Sideleau, p. 389.
19. Ray and Ksir, p. 135.
20. Loebl and Sparatta, p. 392.
21. Kozier and Erb, p. 1362.
22. Loebl and Sparatta, p. 392.

## Chapter 4

1. David Olms, *Addiction Disease*, (Cahokia, Ill.: Gary Whiteaker Corporation, 1993).
2. All interview material taken from author interview with Rob Roddy, December 1995.

## Chapter 5

1. Mary Theresa Webb and Ann Fabean, "Codependence," *Professional Counselor*, April 1993, pp. 32-36.
2. Susan Thenepohn, "Grandchildren of Alcoholics at Risk," *Changes*, September/October 1986, p. 6.
3. Virginia Satir, *Peoplemaking* (Palo Alto, Calif.: Science and Behavior Books, 1972), p. 63.
4. Sharon Wegscheider-Cruse, *Another Chance: Hope and Help for the Alcoholic Family* (Palo Alto, Calif.: Science and Behavior Books, 1981), p. 94.
5. Salvador Minuchin, Bernice Rosman, and Lester Baker, *Psychosomatic Families: Anorexia Nervosa in Context* (Cambridge, Mass: Harvard University Press, 1978), p. 60.
6. Lawrence Clayton, *Coping with a Drug-Abusing Parent* (New York: The Rosen Publishing Group, 1991) pp. 99-122.
7. Dene Stamas, "Signs and Symptoms of Children of Addicts," *The Counselor*, September/October 1986, pp. 22-24

8. Mary Stewart and Lynnzy Orr, "Otherwise Perfect," *Changes*, November/December 1987, pp. 19, 36-37, 48-49.

9. Michael Nichols, *Family Therapy: Concepts and Methods* (New York, Gardner Press, 1984) p. 438.

10. Robert Ackerman, "Dysfunctional Families," *The Counselor*, September/October 1994, pp. 10-14.

11. Eric Bern, *Games People Play* (New York: Random House, 1984) p. 76.

## Chapter 6

1. Rhonda McFarland, *Cocaine* (New York: Rosen, 1991), p. 19.

2. Curtis Janeczek, *Marijuana* (Columbus, Ohio: Healthstar, 1981), pp. 5-6.

3. C. W. Brister, *Pastoral Care* (New York: Harper & Row, 1987), pp. 3-13.

4. Jeanette Kramer, *Family Interfaces* (New York: Brunner/Mazel, 1985), pp. 125-130.

5. Donald Staccia, *A Common Sense Perspective* (Springfield, Ohio: Ascop, 1986), pp. 77-79.

6. Edward Kaufman, *Substance Abuse and Family Therapy*, (Grune & Stratton, 1985), pp. 111-113.

# Further Reading

Avraham, Regina. *The Downside of Drugs.* New York: Chelsea, 1988.

Ball, Jacqueline. *Everything You Need to Know About Drug Abuse,* rev. ed. New York: Rosen, 1992.

Bargmann, Eve, et. al. *Stopping Valium and Ativan, Centrax, Dalmane, Librium, Paxipam, Restoril, Serax, Tranxene, Xanax.* New York: Warner, 1983

Berger, Gilda. *The Pressure to Take Drugs.* New York: Franklin Watts, 1990.

Clayton, Lawrence. *Barbiturates and Other Depressants.* New York: Rosen, 1994.

———. *Coping with a Drug Abusing Parent,* rev. ed. New York: Rosen, 1995.

Edwards, Gabrielle. *Coping with Drug Abuse.* New York: Rosen, 1990.

———. *Drugs on Your Street.* New York: Rosen, 1993.

Estes, Nada, and Edith Heinemann. *Alcoholism: Its Development, Consequences, and Interventions.* Saint Louis. Mo.: C.V. Mosby, 1977.

Green, Bernard. *Goodbye, Blues: Breaking the Tranquilizer Habit the Natural Way.* New York: McGraw-Hill, 1982.

Gordan, Barbara. *I'm Dancing as Fast as I Can.* New York: Harper and Row, 1979.

Hodgkinson, Liz. *Addictions.* Wellingborough, England: Thorsons, 1986.

Hyde, Margaret. *Know About Drugs.* New York: McGraw-Hill, 1979.

Jones, Hardin and Helen. *Sensual Drugs.* London, England: Cambridge, 1978.

Kaplan, Leslie. *Coping with Peer Pressure.* New York: Rosen, 1993.

Kowl, Andrew, ed. *High Times Encyclopedia of Recreational Drugs.* New York: Stonehill, 1978.

Landau, Elaine. *Teenage Drinking.* Hillside, N.J.: Enslow, 1994.

Larson, Earnie. *Old Patterns, New Truths.* New York: Harper/Hazelden, 1989.

Lee, E. *Breaking the Connection.* New York: Messner, 1988.

Leite, Evelyn and Pamela Espeland. *Different Like Me.* Minneapolis: Johnson Institute, 1987.

Levy, S. *Managing the Drugs in Your Life.* New York: McGraw-Hill, 1989.

Madison, Arnold. *Drugs and You.* New York: Messner, 1982.

McFarland, Rhoda. *Coping with Substance Abuse.* New York: Rosen, 1990.

Melville, Joy. *The Tranquilizer Trap and How to Get Out of It.* Glascow, Scotland: Fontana, 1984.

Mothner, I., and A.Weitz. *How to Get Off Drugs.* New York: Rolling Stone, 1985.

O'Brian, Robert and Morris Chafets. *The Encyclopedia of Alcoholism.* New York: Facts on File, 1982.

Smith, Sandra. *Coping with Decision Making.* New York: Rosen, 1994.

——. *Value of Self Esteem.* New York: Rosen, 1991.

Sunshine, L., and J. Wright. *100 Best Treatment Centers for Alcoholism and Drug Abuse.* New York: Avon, 1988.

Weil, Andrew, and Winnifred Rosen. *From Chocolate to Morphine.* Boston, Mass.: Houghton Miffin, 1993.

Weiss, Ann. *Over the Counter Drugs.* New York: Franklin Watts, 1984.

Woods, Geraldine. *Drug and Drug Use.* New York: Franklin Watts, 1986.

# Glossary

**addiction**—Compulsive use of a substance.

**alcohol**—One of the most deadly drugs, it is made from fermented fruit and grains.

**alprazolam**—Generic name for Xanax.

**amphetamine**—A stimulant that speeds up the body and elevates mood.

**analgesic**—Pain medication.

**anxiety**—A state of nervousness.

**Ativan**—Trade name for Lorazepam, a tranquilizer.

**barbiturate**—A downer that slows down the body and depresses the mood. It is often substituted for tranquilizers.

**benzodiazepine**—The most common category of tranquilizer. It includes Librium, Valium, and Xanax.

**blackout**—Drug-induced amnesia.

**blaming**—Psychological defense used by addicts to avoid responsibility for dealing with their addiction.

**CADC**—Certified Alcohol and Drug Counselor.

**centrax**—Generic name for Prazepam, a tranquilizer.

**cocaine**—A stimulant made from the cocoa leaf.

**codependent**—A member of a family with at least one addicted member.

**codependent families**—Families with at least one addicted member.

**coma**—A state of being unconscious. Can be brought about by an overdose.

**cross-tolerance**—Endurance against the effects of a drug, which develops as a consequence of using a similar acting drug.

**dalmame**—Generic name for Flurazepam, a tranquilizer.

**depressant**—A drug that slows down the body and mind.

**denial**—A psychological defense developed by addicts and codependents in order to not know the level of their addiction.

**detox**—Abbreviation for detoxification.

**detoxification**—The process by which a drug is medically withdrawn from an addict.

**diazepam**—The generic name for Valium, a tranquilizer.

**downers**—Another name for depressants.

**drug**—A chemical that artificially stimulates or depresses the mood.

**halcion**—The generic name for Triazolam, a tranquilizer.

**hallucinogen**—A drug that causes the user to see and hear things that are not real.

**heroin**—A depressant from the opium family.

**huffer**—A person who uses inhalants.

**ICADC**—International Certified Alcohol and Drug Counselor.

**inhalant**—A drug that is breathed into the body.

**Librium**—Brand name for chlordiazepoxide, a tranquilizer.

**MAC**—Master Addiction Counselor.

**magic mushrooms**—The name for psychedelic mushrooms, also called "shrooms."

**mainlining**—To inject a drug directly into a vein.

**marijuana**—A drug that is the least powerful of the hallucinogens. Also called "pot," "weed," and "wacky tobaccy." It is frequently used with tranquilizers.

**narcotics**—Depressants from the opium family.

**"nodding-off"**—A symptom of depressant use, it refers to the tendency of users to have difficulty staying awake after using drugs.

**opium**—A narcotic made from the opium poppy.

**overdose**—Taking too much of a drug. This can be fatal.

**paxipam**—The generic name for Halazepam, a tranquilizer.

**psilocybin**—The proper name for mushrooms used by addicts, it is in the hallucinogen class of drugs.

100

**restoril**—The generic name for Temazepam, a tranquilizer.

**sedative**—A class of drug that calms. It includes alcohol, narcotics, barbiturates, and tranquilizers.

**serax**—The generic name for Oxazepam, a tranquilizer.

**side effect**—An unwanted result of drug use.

**speed**—The street name for amphetamine and other stimulants. It is a drug that speeds up the body and elevates the mood.

**tranquilizer**—A class of depressants.

**tranxene**—The generic name for Clorazepate, a tranquilizer.

**Valium**—The brand name for diazepam, a tranquilizer.

**withdrawal**—What the addict experiences when deprived of the drug. Its effects may be physical, emotional, or both.

**Xanax**—The brand name of Alprazolam, a tranquilizer.

# Index